JARROW
THEN & NOW
IN COLOUR

PAUL PERRY

For Angela & Oliver, Anthony & Joanne

First published in 2011

The History Press
The Mill, Brimscombe Port
Stroud, Gloucestershire, GL5 2QG
www.thehistorypress.co.uk

© Paul Perry, 2011

The right of Paul Perry to be identified as the Author
of this work has been asserted in accordance with the
Copyrights, Designs and Patents Act 1988.

British Library Cataloguing in Publication Data.
A catalogue record for this book is available from the British Library.

ISBN 978 0 7524 6316 2

Typesetting and origination by The History Press
Production managed by Jellyfish Print Solutions and manufactured in India

CONTENTS

Acknowledgements   4

About the Author   4

Introduction   5

Jarrow Then & Now   6

ACKNOWLEDGEMENTS

I am indebted to the following people and organisations for their assistance during the preparation of this document: Lawrence Cuthbert, Terry Kelly, Anth & Malcolm Perry, Angela Snowden & Bill Dixon, David Drynan, Local History Department of South Tyneside Libraries and Northeast Press Ltd.

ABOUT THE AUTHOR

Paul Perry was born and raised in Jarrow, where he pursued a career in photography. After learning his profession, he operated from a studio in the town, and it was here that he was introduced to the delights of local history. In 1966 he began amassing a collection of images of his hometown and surrounding area, which is now in excess of 30,000. Paul has written a number of local history books over the last twenty years.

INTRODUCTION

 The history of Jarrow is varied and extensive, and behind its complex character is a somewhat turbulent history. Together with its unique, often-ridiculed character and social status, Jarrow has come through the decades practically unscathed. It has been subject to troubled times ever since the Viking raids of many centuries ago. In its humble beginnings, this former Roman settlement clung to the riverbanks of the ancient river Don. In later years this tiny hamlet took its name from the 'Gyrwe', an ancient tribe who lived there during Bede's time. 'Gyrwe' is derived from the old Anglo-Saxon word for 'mud' or 'fen' and the tribe were known as 'the dwellers on the mudflats' or 'marsh dwellers'. Little is known of the town's development from this time, and what we do know is rather fragmentary until around the fifteenth century, at the time when Jarrow was beginning to make its mark as a town. There is evidence held at Durham Cathedral of coal being raised from a narrow seam close to the banks of the Tyne at Jarrow from as early as 1618, and this breakthrough was to herald the beginning of the town's industrial growth.

  This collection of photographs and captions is not intended to be a definitive history of the town; instead it is hoped that through these unique images from my personal collection and the carefully researched captions, it will provide a glimpse of a town, a sometimes troubled town, which for many years played a dominant role in the industrial heritage of north-east England. Today there is little evidence to show that Jarrow was once a town built on engineering, but there are many Jarovians who have vivid memories of the influence it had on the town. We can only imagine what it was like during the 'dark days' of the 1930s Depression and the difficult times endured by so many, scavenging for coal during the long cold winters. Through those often difficult and challenging times, everyone pulled together, retaining a strong sense of camaraderie and enjoying themselves as best they could, with such pastimes as football, dancing, leek growing and pigeon fancying. Even in the time that has passed since the publication of my last 'trip around the town' in 2008, things have changed: a new bore has been added to the tunnel and the handsome Edwardian grammar school building in Field Terrace has been demolished and replaced with a brand new one. Compared to the towns around us, I tend to think we are bearing up well to the winds of change – better than most in fact. When we look at the bright lights and shiny new shops at the Metro Centre, I am the first to admit that our shopping precincts do look a bit shabby. Harrods and Harvey Nichols may not have opened a branch in Jarrow quite yet, but should either of them consider it, I am sure we would be able to accommodate them. Never mind, come and join me on another jaunt around the town, to see the changes, for better or for worse, for richer or poorer.

Paul Perry, 2011

ELLISON STREET & CIVIC HALL

WITH THE EXCEPTION of the traffic restrictions, the foot of Ellison Street remains largely unchanged. William Dunn & Co., wholesale and retail tobacconists, were the proprietors of Ellison House, to the left of the 1956 photograph below. During the 1980s, this building was converted into a Chinese restaurant. When the 1956 photograph was taken, the shopping centre was under construction, but baker and confectioner Carrick's was the only company attracted to the precincts. Shephards of Gateshead department store traded here for many years, until merging with Joplings of Sunderland, but it was only then that they took property in the Viking Precinct.

Comet, the electrical giant, took over the disused department store until out-of-town shopping in retail parks became fashionable during the 1980s when they moved to larger premises north of the river Tyne. Today the property is occupied by the Department of Employment as a job centre.

ON THE OPPOSITE side of the street we see the Civic Hall, visible to the right of the modern photograph. This building was gifted to the town by shipbuilding magnate Charles Mark Palmer, who laid the foundation stone on 10 October 1877, the day he married Gertrude Montgomery. The building was designed for social gatherings and as reading rooms, and boasted a comprehensive library provided by Palmer at further expense. During the 1950s and '60s the building was used for wedding receptions and similar functions, with 'dinner and dance' being very popular around this time. For several years the Victorian structure was deemed unsafe, and its future hung precariously in the balance. After urgent remedial repair, a further inspection revealed the building had yet again escaped the demolition men and gained another lease of life. Plans are currently being made for the building's future as an entertainment centre.

ALBERT ROAD

IT WAS DURING the early 1970s that the traffic signals in Albert Road were relocated to their present position at the junction of Hill Street and Park Road. Prior to this they were situated 200 yards east, at the junction of Bede Burn Road. This move enabled the authorities to prohibit the movement of traffic further down Albert Road, and re-route the heavy flow of traffic across the newly appointed Humbert Street flyover. The older photograph, by Joseph Connacher, a local photographer, dates from 1953 and formed part of a series of picture postcards. As the modern photograph illustrates, the traffic signals, together with the flyover (just out of shot) ensure the constant movement of traffic, which means fewer hold-ups. The former Jarrow & Hebburn Co-op offices, in the centre, were erected in 1923.

APART FROM THE road markings and the disappearance of the terraced houses to the right of the older image, the scene is very much the same today. The volume of traffic passing this way bears no resemblance to the amount of traffic that passed through when the 1953 photograph was taken. This very busy thoroughfare is one of the main artery roads in and out of town, and remains a major route to South Shields.

BEDE BURN ROAD

JARROW HAS CHANGED significantly during the twentieth century, so much so that parts of the town are barely recognisable today. This part of Bede Burn Road seems to have escaped major changes, if the two identical views on this page are anything to go by, despite being taken almost 100 years apart. Notice the two church spires to the right of the older photograph: the smaller of the two was that of the Congregational church in Station Street, which was consecrated on 1 May 1871, built at a cost of £1,600 and demolished during the eventful 1960s to make way for further town planning. The larger spire is Christ Church, which has dominated the Jarrow skyline since it was added to the church in 1882. In around 1970, the town council,

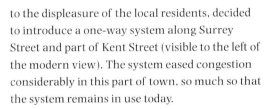

to the displeasure of the local residents, decided to introduce a one-way system along Surrey Street and part of Kent Street (visible to the left of the modern view). The system eased congestion considerably in this part of town, so much so that the system remains in use today.

EVEN THOUGH THE 1970s one-way system was originally put in place as a temporary measure, it proved to be the perfect solution for relieving the ever-increasing congestion in this part of town. During the latter part of the nineteenth century, when the sought-after houses in Bede Burn Road became ready for occupancy, a by-law was passed by the town council which dictated that no public houses were to be opened within the vicinity, and that all such establishments were to be contained within the town centre, in order to keep the area strictly residential. The council made an exception, however, and provided private facilities here for the major political parties. Although the Borough of Jarrow Corporation was disbanded in 1974, the by-law is still adhered to.

WESTERN ROAD

AS INDUSTRY AND the economy grew steadily in Jarrow, so did the need for a reliable transport service in order to shuttle the men back and forth to work. The electric tramcar was looked upon favourably as similar systems in other towns had proved to be very efficient. Any system in Jarrow would have to be efficient, convenient and economically viable for it to operate smoothly. Many hundreds of men and boys were involved in the arduous task of laying mile upon mile of track in readiness for the new tram service which was scheduled for trials in 1906. Contractors and

sub-contractors worked relentlessly for six years to lay the 17 miles of track from Tyne Dock to Western Road where the service would terminate. Passengers wishing to travel beyond this point could do so with the aid of horse-drawn buses that operated in conjunction with the tram service. Western Road, shown in the older image of the track nearing completion, had a plentiful supply of shops and was a heavily built-up area of the town.

TODAY THE SHOPS have gone, as have the hundreds of terraced houses in Palmer Street and the surrounding area. The vast site, on which Palmer's yard once reigned supreme, has now been converted into an industrial park. This came after several years of geology reports and soil analysis that were required because the earth beneath was so heavily polluted from almost 150 years of industrial activity. Today there is no evidence whatsoever that there was a tram service in Jarrow. The old tracks were either buried or raised and sold for scrap.

CHURCH BANK

IN TIMES GONE by this part of Jarrow was as industrious as the main body of the town. In fact, it was here that the town's industrial past began. The chemical industry emerged as early as 1845 with the production of sulphur for match heads. Many industries followed over the subsequent years, though the only survivors now are specialists in the timber trade and an oil storage depot. In 1785 Simon Temple, whose reputation as an industrial giant rather precedes him, chose a spot close by to build a fine residence that he called Jarrow Hall. It was from this old house that he organised his business

empire, which began with shipbuilding and progressed latterly to coal mining. As time passed, Jarrow Hall was left unoccupied and eventually lay derelict for many years. It was saved from total dereliction by Jarrow Corporation, who converted it into a museum. Today it forms an annexe to Bede's World visitor centre. The older view of Church Bank is from around 1910, when it was the main trunk road to and from South Shields before the completion of the modern network of roads linking the Tyne Tunnel.

THE BIGGEST CIVIL engineering project the country has seen for several years is the second Tyne Tunnel, which was completed in 2011. The original tunnel had been opened by Her Majesty the Queen in 1967, and while it was adequate for the traffic of the time, there is now much more traffic than it was designed to cope with. The new tunnel opened to the public at midnight on 25 February 2011 and the first car to enter it was the all-electric Nissan Leaf. The official opening will be in 2012. This (still busy) road was originally the main route for the tram service that operated from 1906 to 1929 from Tyne Dock to Western Road in Jarrow. Evidence of the tram service is visible in the older of the accompanying photographs.

15

PALMER'S SHIPYARD

IN 1851 CHARLES Mark Palmer began his shipbuilding business with his brother George under the name of Palmer Bros & Co. It was a modest beginning like most other businesses of the time. The days of wooden ships had not yet gone, but the brothers' instinct told them that they were rapidly coming to a close. Their first vessel in 1851 was a mere tugboat, but very soon they went on to build far greater projects. In 1852 the *John Bowes* was launched, a vessel that had the privilege of being the world's first iron-screw collier. After a remarkable eighty-two years, she ran aground off the northern coast of Spain. The Palmer success story was aided by the use of a steel 'rolling' process, and for this the yard operated 8 miles of internal railway and boasted the biggest foundry on the east coast along with an impressive galvanising plant. The four unique German-built

cantilevered overhead cranes that towered over the yard's 140 acres and indeed the whole of Jarrow, were constructed to Palmer's own specifications. These works were among the world's giants, and employed the majority of the town's male working population. As had long been the boast of Jarovians, Palmer's took in iron ore at one end of the yard and sailed it out in the form of a ship at the other. Palmer's survived many troubled times, and several downturns in the shipbuilding industry, and would rise like the phoenix from the ashes on every occasion. But it was the Depression of the 1930s that finally signalled the end for this well-respected and world-famous shipyard, which was responsible for the construction of in excess of 1,000 vessels. Palmer's gates finally closed in 1934, heralding the end of shipbuilding in Jarrow. The land it once occupied lay dormant for many years until the Consett Iron Co. utilised part of it for their operation until the 1980s.

TODAY NONE OF the industrial giants that hugged this once busy waterway survive, and in their place are several smaller factories and warehouses on the Viking Business Park, a modern industrial estate. Northumbria Police are also active in the area with their marine division and diving school.

ELLISON STREET

AT ONE TIME, Ellison Street covered an area of approximately
half a mile, from the junction with Ormonde Street to the
other end of town where it merged with St John's Terrace,
close to Greenbank Villas. Today it comes to an abrupt halt
at Station Street, where the Humbert Street flyover begins.
This flyover was designed to replace the traffic signals at
Carrick's Corner where Albert Road meets Bede Burn Road,
thus ensuring free-flowing traffic to and from South Shields
and the Tyne Tunnel approach roads. Not one single house
remains in this once heavily populated street. Today the upper
section of Ellison Street is generally given over to shopping,
while the lower section is used mainly by the four major
banks and offices, much the same as it was in the older of the
two photographs, in 1888. Maxwells have traded here in the
former Scotts stationery shop for some time; prior to this their
business operated from Bede Burn Road.

DURING THE 1950s, Jarrow became the first town in the
country to become a smokeless zone, chosen because of its
industrial heritage. After many years of heavy engineering,

some of the town's finest buildings were blackened with sooty deposits – a direct result of the many shipyards that dominated the river Tyne. The authorities were concerned about the effect that this industrial pollution was having on the health of the townsfolk, and the 1970s saw the introduction of 'operation clean up' when all the notable buildings in Jarrow were freed of this industrial grime. Today the shipyards are no longer a feature of our town and consequently the air that we breathe is not as contaminated as it once was.

ARNDALE CENTRE

AS THE SHOPPING centre slowly rose from the ground, Jarrow Corporation predicted huge crowds travelling into town. Provision had been made for 200 parking spaces behind the centre – not very many by today's standards – but in 1961, at the time of the older photograph, our streets and roads were not as cluttered with vehicles as they are today. To accommodate the expected influx of traffic, alterations had to be made to some roads in central Jarrow. Grange Road almost doubled in width, while major changes occurred in Monkton Road. Perhaps the most significant change of the era was the removal of a huge chunk of the junction of Grange Road with Ellison Street. Just how much was removed can be seen in a glance by looking at the modern photograph.

BEFORE THE SHOPPING centre was built this part of town was largely given over to housing, spread over four streets: Ellison Street, Caledonian Road, Charles Street and Hibernian Road. This area covered 12 acres, and most of these houses were occupied by families who worked in the shipyards. In 1955 the area was cleared to make way for the shopping centre.

BEDE BURN ROAD

ANOTHER INTERESTING VIEW of Bede Burn Road, this time at a point closer to the town centre. L&N Stores, to the right of the 1950s photograph, ceased trading here in the 1960s. The building that it occupied was found to be structurally insecure and was demolished shortly afterwards, and

the land was planted with shrubs and bushes. On the opposite side of the street there was a small but varied assortment of shops – enough to satisfy the daily needs of local residents.

IN 1954, WHEN the older of the accompanying photographs was taken, practically every major street in Jarrow had its own corner shop. There are too many to list here, but anyone familiar with the town will have fond memories of their personal favourite. These emporiums stocked what seemed to be an endless supply of everything from gas mantles to pipe cleaners, and almost everything in-between. I am not suggesting that L&N Stores was a corner shop, on the contrary, it was in fact one of the country's leading grocers. L&N was the trading name of the London & Newcastle Tea Company who purchased the Home & Colonial chain of stores just after the Second World War. The company traded from premises in Grange Road after the opening of the shopping centre in 1961, and changed their name to Fine Fare later in the decade.

VIKING SCULPTURE

COUNCILLORS, LOCAL DIGNITARIES and the people of Jarrow listen intently to the words of Mayor Councillor Violet Hope as she unveils a sculpture of two Vikings on 19 February 1962, sculpted by C.M. Davidson of Orpington in Kent. The statues were donated and presented to the town council by Chippendale & Co. (the investors and planners who owned the shopping centre)

to commemorate the official opening of the Arndale shopping centre. The sculpture represents two Viking invasions on Jarrow – or Gyrwy as it was then called – in AD 794 and again in AD 870. These Scandinavian warriors were more than just raiders; they were also traders and colonists who left an enduring mark on Britain. The Vikings attacked the country's holy places, and the monasteries at Wearmouth, Lindisfarne and Jarrow were no exception. They slaughtered the monks and carried off what few possessions they had. Their well-designed longboats, coupled with strong northerly winds, meant they were well equipped to come and go as they pleased and to loot and pillage in countless hit-and-run raids. When these controversial sculptures first appeared in Jarrow, locals were horrified at the unsightly pair of new residents. As the years passed however, people have warmed to the warriors' presence.

WITH THE PASSING of time, the elements have taken their toll on the jolly green giants. In 2005 and at a cost of £10,000 the sculpture was removed, renovated and put back into its original position among the people of Jarrow. It seems rather bizarre that we would commemorate invasions to our shores with these marauding murderers. Bede's World in the east end of the town is a museum and visitor centre that houses a realistic recreation and example of early Viking activity and Anglo Saxon life. This Viking name lives on in the town centre too, where there are many businesses bearing it.

ALBERTA CLUB

THE OLDER OF the two photographs is the Alberta Working Men's Club in Albert Road in 1978. This former residence was built in 1890, complete with stables and servants' quarters, for estate agent William George Harris. He resided here (it is thought) until 1923, when the house was purchased by a physician who later retired to a smaller property in 1935, the same year that the house underwent conversion for use as a club that traded at the premises for forty-four years. As the membership steadily grew, so did the need for larger premises. A site once occupied by Gaudies bakery in Grant Street became available and, after planning permission was granted, building commenced on the new club in 1979. The old club premises were demolished to make way for Kingfisher Lodge, the residential block in the picture above. The architects of the block have made some effort to design the building in a similar style to that of its predecessor.

VIRTUALLY EVERY TOWN in the country had an assortment of committee-run working men's clubs, and Jarrow was no exception. Originally, as the name suggests, these were men-only domains, and it is only within the last fifty years or so that women have been allowed into the inner sanctum of these members-only establishments, and even then they were often only allowed into certain areas of the club. During the 1960s, these clubs became big business and attracted big-name entertainers. As their popularity grew so did the need for bigger premises. Several of the more wealthy establishments sought sites to build bigger and better venues, some seating as many as 750. Quality entertainment was offered on a weekly basis and food and drinks were also on offer at very competitive prices. Bingo was another of the attractions and was played most nights of the week. The success of these clubs was a far cry from the tiny, draughty, dimly-lit, often one-roomed converted houses similar to the Alberta Club (pictured below) where the CIU movement began in 1862. Sadly nothing lasts forever. Towards the closing years of the 1990s, these once very popular entertainment centres were rapidly becoming most unfashionable, with the masses seeking other venues to spend their time and money. Very few of these clubs survive today, and some of those that have are struggling in the fight for survival in the current economic climate.

ST PAUL'S CHURCH

ST PAUL'S CHURCH, most of which dates from the seventh century, holds the distinction of being one of the oldest buildings in the country. This we can ascertain from two stones found in the church in 1782 that dedicated the little church to St Paul on the 9 Kalends of May in the fifteenth year of the reign of King Egfrith. The relics have been preserved and mounted in an arch between the chancel and the nave of the church. It has been claimed for many centuries that Jarrow was the site of a

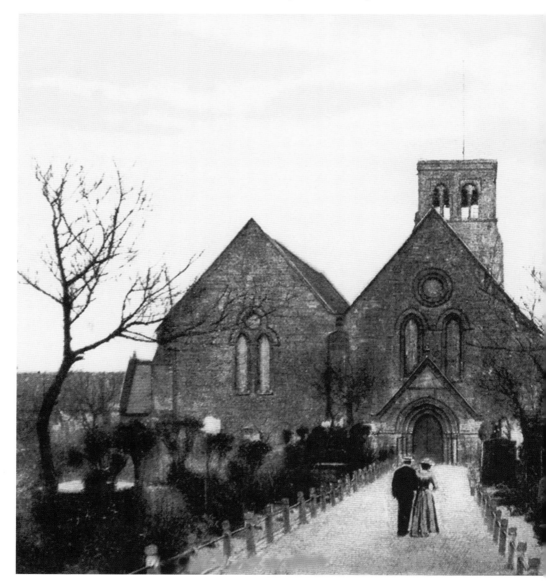

Roman fort and settlement, and at the same time disclaimed by historians throughout history. However, it is believed that two Roman inscriptions were found during church renovations. This is supported by the nearby discovery of two square pavements made from Roman brick, fashioned in the style of Roman masonry dating from AD 80.

THIS ANCIENT PLACE of worship is as popular as ever with worshippers and tourists alike, and attracts thousands of pilgrims from far-reaching corners of the earth who wish to visit the place where the Venerable Bede himself worshipped. A crudely built little chair sits somewhat awkwardly within the church, and for many centuries was attributed to Bede, but recent carbon dating revealed that the simple little chair dates from the eleventh century – almost 500 years after the death of the great man. But the legend will live on forever as a relic and a reminder of another age.

JARROW GRAMMAR SCHOOL

THE FIRST SCHOOL in Jarrow, the Bede Parochial, was situated close to St Paul's church in the east end of the town and dated from 1840. This was followed by the Ellison Church of England School on a stretch of land close to Ellison Street in 1863. In 1872 St Bede's Boys' School was opened at Low Jarrow, at a time when education facilities were becoming more organised. This school was in use until 1914, when a purpose-built school capable of accommodating 700 pupils became available in Harold Street. The Hedworth, Monkton and Jarrow School Board came into force in 1872; prior to this the education of children was at the discretion of parents or guardians.

At the time any building with four walls and a roof was deemed adequate for educating children. The first school to open after the Jarrow School Board made education compulsory was the Grange Board School in a disused theatre in Drury Lane.

JARROW GRAMMAR SCHOOL (pictured) was built in 1911, and served the town for almost 100 years. It ceased to be a grammar school in 1975 when it became Springfield Comprehensive after a merger of Springfield and Hedworthfield schools. From this time it became known as Jarrow School, and was situated in the former grammar school building in Field Terrace. The title was chosen as a result of a competition to choose an inspirational name, and in 2007 the school became a specialist engineering college. The original school buildings were demolished in 2010, after the recent construction and opening of a replacement school close by in Field Terrace, which is large enough to accommodate 990 pupils. The site of the former school buildings is currently being developed into a comprehensive sports facility.

BEN LOMOND HOTEL

OF THE FIFTY-FOUR public houses within the town centre, the Ben Lomond Hotel was by far the grandest establishment of all. The older image is from the 1930s, at a time when the Victorian building was used as a residential hotel, which is how it remained until the 1970s. While the exterior of the building always looked as good as it did when it was first built, the interior was neglected and eventually began to need serious attention. Local entrepreneur Derek Armstrong, who owned both the County Hotel and the Cavalier Club, rented the building from Scottish & Newcastle Breweries, who owned it. He restored it to a very high standard and renamed it The Viking. By 1995, and many lessees later, this grand old building had once again slipped into a

state of disrepair and was deemed to be a white elephant that no one wanted. It was feared that the mighty building was to be razed to the ground, much to the displeasure of Jarovians. Brewing giants Wetherspoon's owned the property briefly during the 1990s when they refurbished and restored the building, and reverted it back to its original name, Ben Lomond Hotel.

OF THOSE FIFTY-FOUR public houses in and around the town centre during the 1930s, only six remain. The population of Jarrow at this time was around 30,000, a level at which it remains today. These public houses flourished for many years, catering for the hundreds of men who toiled in the shipyards. The major employer was Palmer's shipyard, whose employees worked two twelve-hour shifts around the clock, seven days a week. One pub in particular, the Forresters Arms, opened its doors for business daily at 5.30am, serving mulled rum to the Palmer workforce just prior to their shift at 6.00am. The success of the Forresters Arms was mainly due to its proximity to Palmer's main gate.

ORMONDE STREET

THERE ARE MANY photographs available of Ormonde Street as it was in the closing years of the nineteenth century up until the 1960s, when the original buildings were demolished. There was always activity of one kind or another in this bustling street, which was the busiest in town

as far as shopping was concerned. The only building to escape the demolition men was the former Burton building, which still survives and is now a carpet store. The entrance directly in front of it, seen in the older of the two photographs, gave access to the market square, which was centred around an old Victorian theatre, also demolished in 1963.

UP UNTIL 2002, the former Theatre Royal and Market Square sites were occupied by North Court, a modern municipal housing complex dating from 1963. At this time Jarrow was in a transitional state as slum clearance got underway, and new houses were springing up almost overnight. Twelve years later, in 1977, the houses were refurbished at enormous cost to South Tyneside Council. By 1987, the houses had once again fallen into disrepair, and again the council rescued the ailing complex. Eventually, the houses were demolished and the 5-acre site upon which they stood was sold to property developers. Once again the land was utilised to its full capacity with almost 200 smart new private houses built. F.W. Woolworth has, it seems, been in Jarrow since the beginning of time; originally situated in Ormonde Street in this photograph from 1953, it remained here until 1961, when the company vacated the site in favour of a modern purpose-built unit in the Arndale Centre, where it remained until its demise in 2008.

ARNDALE SHOPPING CENTRE

WHEN THE ARNDALE Centre opened for trading in 1961, there was an abundance of shops catering for everyone's needs. There was enough business for four major furniture stores: Smiths Ltd who manufactured furniture in Jarrow; the Bede Furnishing Co.; Jarrow & Hebburn Co-operative Society and Hardy's (pictured). Today furniture shops in Jarrow are non-existent, forcing shoppers to travel further afield if they want to make a purchase. However, apart from a cosmetic makeover and shops changing ownership once or twice, this view remains exactly the same as it did when the photograph was taken almost fifty years ago.

FROM AROUND 1860 onwards, the Jarrow skyline was peppered with church spires of all denominations – that was until wandering bands of so-called demolition experts appeared. Sadly, one by one they were razed to the ground within a very short period of time during the 1960s. Some of these beautiful buildings with their imposing spires had seen better days, and perhaps dwindling congregations and ever-rising costs were also to blame for their downfall. However, services at Christ Church (pictured) remained very well attended and as a consequence it was saved from a similar fate. Today the church is still serving the community almost 145 years after its consecration.

MASONIC HALL
AND TOWN HALL

THE OLDER OF these images was taken at the junction of Ellison Street and Grange Road on what seems to be a windy day in 1945. The foundation stone for the Masonic Hall to the left of the photograph was laid by the grand master, Brother George Spain, on 21 April 1881. The proceedings commenced with an emergency lodge meeting held in the Mechanics Institute in Ellison Street. The brothers, dressed in full Masonic regalia, walked in procession to the stone laying ceremony in Grange Road. The party was led by the band of the Durham Engineers Volunteers. A similar ceremony took place

on 15 February 1882 at the official opening of the hall. The building to the right of the hall is the office of the Sunderland & South Shields Water Co. and today is used by an estate agent, which can be seen in the modern image, taken from the same perspective. The building in the centre is the town hall, which dates from 1902. The formation of Jarrow Council came about long before the town hall was built. The first municipal election of eighteen councillors for the recently created town wards occurred on 10 August 1875, with the swearing-in ceremony and the signing of the declarations taking place at the Board of Health Offices in Grange Road on 18 August.

FROM 1902 ALL decisions concerning the town and its people were made in the council chambers of the recently appointed town hall, and this remained the case until 1974 when Jarrow was amalgamated with South Shields, Hebburn and the Boldons to form the Metropolitan Borough of South Tyneside.

SWIMMING BATHS

PUBLIC BATHING FACILITIES were available in Jarrow even before the swimming baths in Walter Street were opened in 1911, mainly due to the lack of such facilities in private homes. Washhouses were common up and down the country in the nineteenth and the first quarter of the twentieth century. This custom goes back to Roman times and beyond, which we can ascertain from the ruins of the many Roman settlements. The advent of modern housing in Jarrow came in 1920, when many houses with private bathing facilities were constructed in

the town's garden suburb Primrose; a luxury few people in Jarrow had experienced, having survived for many years in damp, cramped conditions – very often a family of five had no other option than to share a single bedroom. The days of wandering down the back yard to 'fetch a pail of water' were coming to an end. Some of the older properties in central Jarrow were still without amenities until they were demolished in the late 1950s.

THE WELCOME FESTIVAL Flats, a complex of eighty-four sought-after dwellings in High Street came along in 1952 and were looked upon as luxury living. By 1965 slum clearance in the central area was nearing completion. The council wasted no time in the construction of two- and three-bedroom houses in all parts of the town, and by 1963 the council had built and allocated no fewer than 5,000 houses. These smart new private houses in Walter Street on the site of the former swimming baths typifies living conditions in modern-day Jarrow.

ARNDALE HOUSE

IT WAS THE partnership of Arnott and Chippendale that dreamed up the name Arndale and who were probably the first to become involved with 1960s-style inner-city shopping malls. Consequently, the white four-storey building in the centre of the older photograph was named Arndale House. The first two floors of the building were utilised as offices, while the upper floors were given over for use as Club Franchi, an exclusive night spot and the brainchild of Italian brothers Franchi and Valente. Continental-style nightclubs were fashionable and appeared in most towns and cities during the 1960s, with major stars from the world of entertainment as the main attraction. Meanwhile in nearby South Shields, the Baily Organisation was gathering strength with a chain of these clubs, the first of which was the Latino.

OTHER NIGHTSPOTS WITHIN the organisation were La Dolce Vita and Cavendish in Newcastle, and Club Fiesta in Stockton. Another very successful club in South Shields was La Strada but this was not part of the Baily Organisation. These clubs, with their exotic sounding names, seemed to conjure up visions of far away places.

The public were attracted by five-star cabarets from the far-reaching corners of the entertainment industry, and it gave them the opportunity to dress up and sample the good life, to wine and dine in a style to which they were unaccustomed. The high costs of running these establishments and

the high fees for the international stars who entertained in them, was reflected in the over-the-top prices charged at the bar. Eventually cabaret became dated and unfashionable. During the late 1970s, the clubs converted to discos, which attracted a much younger audience, but alas this scene died out a short time later in the 1980s. Today the many wine bars in the region seem to be the places to be seen.

VIKING PRECINCT

AMERICAN-STYLE TEN-PIN BOWLING centres were more popular in the south of the country, but were eventually to drift north by the 1960s. In 1962 Jarrow was chosen as the location for the first of such centres, which was to be located beneath Arndale House. The popularity of the pastime grew and leagues were formed as the craze swept the North East, with bowling alleys seemingly springing up overnight. In 1964, the Dogs Bowl was opened in South Shields on the site of the former greyhound stadium and this was followed by Excel bowling centres in Sunderland, Gateshead and Newcastle. By the late 1960s, with the game rapidly losing its popularity, the North East was overcrowded with bowling alleys. In Jarrow, the first to open was the first to close – which it did in

1968 after just six years. The remainder closed in a short space of time, with the exception of those in Newcastle and Sunderland, which today are enjoying a revival along with recently opened centres in the Metro Centre and in nearby Washington.

DURING THE 1970S, the Arndale Centre was greatly in need of urgent attention just fifteen years after it had opened. Arndale House (pictured) was completely refurbished both inside and out, to the extent that its whole exterior was replaced with coloured glass, which improved its appearance considerably. The 1980s saw another major refit and a name change to the 'Viking Centre'. Initially the centre was owned and managed by the Arndale Property Trust Co., but was bought in the late 1970s by the group Town & Cities, and was then owned by P&O Properties from around 1990. Today Zurich Insurance manages the yet again renovated centre. After the demise of the Excel bowling centre in 1968, the vast empty space it left became an ideal site for the Presto supermarket and remained so until this part of the centre was demolished along with Arndale House. The site was cleared from the old arcade down to Chapel Road; Morrisons' supermarket was built on the vacant site and has most certainly improved this part of town, both cosmetically and financially. Cambrian Street and the barren land on which the former Festival Flats once stood were converted into a much needed and very welcome car park. The sculpture in the centre of the modern photograph represents a 'spring washer' as a reminder of the town's links with engineering.

CENTRAL JARROW, LOOKING EAST

DURING THE EARLY part of the twentieth century, Jarrow accommodated a moderate influx of Irish immigrant workers, who were attracted to the town and the work it had to offer. Around the same time, though not in such numbers as our Irish cousins, a small number of Italian families were beginning to settle in north-east England. Salvatore Rea and his wife Martha originally came to England from Arpino in southern Italy, and arrived in Middlesbrough in 1898, where they resided for a period of seven years. After a further year in Newcastle they decided that Jarrow was where they wanted to make their living selling ice cream, which they did for many years. During the 1930s, in what would seem an unlikely combination while running an ice cream parlour, Salvatore, assisted by his eldest son Dominic, busied himself with a demolition business, which he operated from a garage in Pitt Street, pictured right.

THE MODERN PHOTOGRAPH shows clearly how the landscape has changed over the last forty or so years. Long gone are the tumbledown makeshift garages and the affectionately-named 'rag shop' in Pitt Street. These were demolished in favour of the

much-needed houses mentioned earlier in the book. The building to the right of the centre is the
Ex-servicemen's working men's club which was relocated here from a site in Grange Road in 1962
as it was deemed that the former club was too small for the ever increasing membership. The white
chimney-like structure is one of two ventilating shafts for the first of the road tunnels opened
in 1967; the other is on the north side of the river. To the left of this we see cranes and heavy
machinery assembling in readiness to excavate a second Tyne Tunnel and a closer look reveals that
the piles for the £260 million project are already in position at the water's edge.

BUS DEPOT

BY THE 1940s people were becoming more dependent upon public transport, there were fleets of buses and the number of destinations available were growing daily, with journeys to all parts of north-east England possible. Newcastle and South Shields operated trolleybuses – an electric system powered by overhead cables. This was a very clean, swift and economical service, though limited to inner towns and cities. The trolleys were discontinued during the 1950s, in favour of the more modern and versatile motor buses, which were garaged locally at South Shields. The need for more depots became evident as the fleet multiplied. The Jarrow station came along during

the 1950s, to a convenient site in the centre of town. By the 1990s a depot of this size was deemed uneconomical as more passengers were using the Metro system.

SINCE THE 1950S, Jarrow seems to have been in a constant state of repair and refurbishment. As fast as town centre buildings were being demolished new ones were rapidly springing up. A purpose-built Kwik Save supermarket was under construction in 1993, on the site of the former bus depot. Simultaneously plans were being prepared for a more modern, passenger friendly bus depot close by, if somewhat smaller than the original. This was designed to serve the region and operate in conjunction with the Metro, a rapid transit system. Kwik Save was originally founded in Wales in 1959 under its original name of Value Foods. The name change came about in the early 1960s. The successful company was floated on the London Stock Exchange in 1970 under the banner of Kwik Save Discount Food Group Ltd. The company merged with Somerfield in 1998, and was eventually taken over by The Co-operative Food. Somerfield ceased trading in Jarrow soon after the arrival of Morrisons' superstore in 2001. After extensive refurbishment the former supermarket is now occupied by Home Bargains.

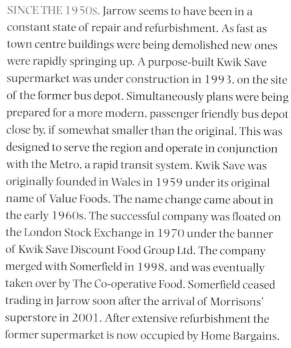

ST JOHN'S TERRACE

IT WAS THE well-heeled of the town who resided in this once well-off area of Jarrow. Most of the elegant old houses in St John's Terrace were home to the medical practitioners who served the people of Jarrow for most of their working lives. Dr Laydon operated a surgery from here, as did Dr Sprague and Dr Isabel Forster. The latter two later moved to a larger establishment in Suffolk Street and then on to the purpose-built Mayfield Medical Centre in Park Road, so called because it was built on the site of Mayfield Girls' School after its demolition in the 1970s. The telephone exchange was contained within the wall to the left of the older photograph. In 1955, when this photograph was taken, it was operated by the general post office (GPO). Today the exchange, now

fully automated, remains in the same place but is managed by British Telecom.

THE ORIGIN OF Ellison Street was very close to the river Tyne, and terminated at its junction with St John's Terrace, making it one of the town's longest thoroughfares. A bus terminal was erected during the 1950s and Ellison Street was used as one of the major roads for this busy bus route in and out of town. Prior to the arrival of the terminal, buses were parked at designated intervals along the upper part of Ellison Street, which became somewhat congested. It was from here that passengers would board the service required. At the completion of the Humbert Street flyover, the flow of traffic was interrupted in Ellison Street at its junction with Station Street, and as a consequence the bus route along St John's Terrace was terminated. As the flyover continued to nearby Monkton Terrace, St John's Terrace was severed rather abruptly as can be seen in these two contrasting images. Although the parish of St Bede was founded around 1859, the church (pictured) didn't appear until two years later in 1861, and will celebrate its 150th anniversary on 27 December 2011.

MONKTON VILLAGE

THE VILLAGE OF Monkton is derived from the name 'monk's town', for it was to here that the brethren fled after the desecration of their monastery at Donmouth in the ninth century, while the remainder went into hiding as far afield as Chester-le-Street. It is only in the last fifty or so years that the appearance of this picturesque little village has changed considerably. For centuries it was exactly as we see it in this picture from 1898, with just one road.

NEW HOUSES HAVE gradually sprung up on the periphery of this ancient village, which many years ago was nothing more than cornfields. The Monkton Leek, Floral and Vegetable Society was founded in 1864, and although the membership has fluctuated from time to time, the enthusiasm of its members has ensured that the society is one of the most popular in the region; it is also thought to be the oldest in the country. The Lord Nelson Inn (pictured above) is the current host of the annual autumn show. The popularity of this event is evident through the huge crowds it attracts.

MERCANTILE
ENGINEERING COMPANY

SHIP REPAIRING BECAME big business in Jarrow and was one of the town's major industries, as the world's fleets steadily grew. By the late nineteenth century there was high demand for a ship repair yard close to the mouth of the Tyne and specialising in the repair and refit of colliers and cargo boats. In 1885 the Mercantile Dry Dock & Engineering Co. filled this gap and spent almost 100 years repairing and refitting virtually every type of craft from the waterways of

the world. As the business expanded so did the facilities, and by 1908 a third dry dock became available, thus shortening the queues of ships awaiting a berth, which often lay as many as five deep along the quays. By 1955, as bigger and faster ships were built, the need for a fourth dry dock became evident and the monster No. 4 dock was completed by 1960. This was fitted with the latest equipment, making it the most comprehensive dry dock on the Tyne, able to accommodate and cope with the biggest craft of the day. From the mid 1960s, the yard changed ownership several times and as ships became more reliable, fewer passed this way, causing a rapid decline in the industry and the closure of the yard in 1981.

THE OPERATION WAS mothballed for some considerable time, with a view to a successor re-investing in the crippled yard, but this was all to no avail. The contents, machinery, and the total assets of the company, which was owned by the Tyne Ship Repair Group at the time of closure, were auctioned off and the four enormous dry docks were subsequently backfilled. In excess of 500 personnel were employed by the company when it was solvent in its heyday during the 1950s and '60s when the order books were very healthy indeed. Little of the former repair yard survives any more, which is illustrated in the more recent of these photographs. The yard eventually closed in 1981 and today Cemex Aggregates occupy the site.

RAILWAY STATION

RAILWAY STATIONS UP and down the country had a style of their own, and were instantly recognisable, as were the old water board buildings. The older of these two photographs was taken from Grant Street in 1948. The station building dates from 1872, but prior to this the station was in Wylam Street. The draughty Victorian building, complete with flickering gaslights, survived on the Newcastle to South Shields line for almost a century, until it was considered past its best and subsequently demolished in the late 1960s. British Rail had an abundance of 'scammel trucks' throughout the country, much the same as the one parked outside the main entrance to the station. These highly efficient and adaptable three-wheeled vehicles delivered goods and rail freight around the neighbourhood for many years.

ALL THAT REMAINS of the station are the two original platforms. Today the scene has changed dramatically, yet it remains a very busy passenger link for the Tyne & Wear Metro. Phase one on the yellow line operates between South Shields and Whitley Bay on the north side of the river, via a network of stations in and around Newcastle city centre, and was officially opened by Her Majesty Queen Elizabeth II in 1980. Phase two of the publicly owned system was extended as far as Newcastle Airport; prior to this the airport was only accessible by road, thus making this extension invaluable to thousands of commuters. The Metro expansion programme continued with a further extension from Sunderland to Newcastle airport, which became available in 2002 on the green line, again passing through Newcastle city centre. Nexus, who operate the rapid transit system on 48 miles of track, had a £40 million turnover between 2009 and 2010. From its inauguration in 1980 up to 2008, the service had provided no less than 40 million public journeys. Recently, 'named and shamed' boards have appeared on station walls in order to combat fare evasion.

PARK ROAD

WHEN THE HOUSES in Park Road were constructed towards the end of the nineteenth century, photography was still very much in its infancy. In some early photographs (like the one shown here), artists would sketch in details that were not picked up by the camera. This is illustrated by the chimneys of Palmer's works, to the left of the older photograph – one in a series of picture postcards issued around the turn of the century. The building on the extreme right was the Chapel of the Good Shepherd. As is illustrated in the modern photograph, the chapel, which was demolished during the 1970s, was replaced with private housing.

UP UNTIL THE mid 1970s, the Labour Party headquarters were situated in this picturesque Victorian thoroughfare, along with Jarrow Trades & Labour working men's club, which was sadly another victim of the recent economic recession

and followed what has become the modern trend and gone out of business. This occurred in 2009 after several attempts to rescue the ailing establishment. When this club was thriving back in the 1960s, an extension was added to the building to create a concert room, but in 2010 this part of the now-unused club in Kent Street was demolished. The main part of this structurally sound and handsome building survived the bulldozers and it has undergone an extensive conversion into luxury apartments. The area once covered by the concert room is now a car park.

CHRIST CHURCH

WITH THE EXCEPTION of the removal of the Longmore memorial drinking fountain and the demolition of the houses behind it, this scene remains almost exactly as it was a century ago. The fountain was relocated to a prime site in Springwell Park in 1921, but no one seems able to recollect what became of the horse trough that stood alongside it. Christ Church, in the centre, was erected and consecrated in 1869. At this time religion played a major part in the lives of the people of Jarrow, which is evident in that at the turn of the century there were no fewer than twelve churches and chapels of all denominations within the confines of the town centre, all in close proximity to

one another. Today just four of the original twelve remain, the others perhaps victims of dwindling congregations.

NO MATTER WHERE you are in Jarrow the imposing spire of Christ Church is visible from almost everywhere. In 1863, prior to the building of the church, evening services took place in the local schools and in 1868 the Revd John Bee was appointed first rector of the new parish of Jarrow Grange. In 1869, with the financial support of Sir Walter and Lady James, the church was built and consecrated on 5 October the same year. The tower and spire with six bells were added to the church in 1882. The Golden Jubilee was celebrated in November 1919 when Dr Moule, bishop of Durham, dedicated two additional bells as a memorial to those men who fell in the 1914–18 war, making a full peal of eight. No fewer than fifty-nine rectors and curates have served Christ Church's parishioners to the present day. An interesting note from an extract of the churchwardens' statement for 1883 reads; 'Income £165 with just £20 deducted for a whole year's heating and lighting.' The Ben Lomond Hotel, to the right of these two contrasting images, was a purpose-built hotel, which dates from the end of the nineteenth century. This was one of two such establishments in the central area, the other being the North Eastern Hotel in Railway Street. It was within these two fine buildings that influential guests and potential clients of Sir Charles Mark Palmer resided and were entertained during their many visits to Jarrow. Much to the disgust of many local residents the Ben Lomond changed its name to The Viking in the late 1960s. When Wetherspoon's purchased the building as a going concern in the 1990s, the name reverted back to the Ben Lomond, much to the delight of the once discontented townsfolk. The North Eastern Hotel was demolished some years ago, but the Ben Lomond still trades as a public house under the management of brewing giants Greene King, but is no longer residential.

CHAYTOR STREET

AS IN MOST towns and cities, streets and buildings were sometimes named in honour of former councillors and eminent citizens. Chaytor Street, pictured here, was named in memory of Alfred Henry Chaytor, a New Zealander who inherited Jarrow Hall from his uncle, Drewett Ormonde Drewett (it is from this man that we get the names of Ormonde Street and the Drewett Playing Fields). Chaytor Street has changed considerably over the last fifty or so years and today it forms part of the ring road around Jarrow, removing the burden of heavy traffic from the town centre. St Peter's church (right) was consecrated on 29 June 1881. Originally the 400-seat church boasted a 117ft spire, but this was demolished during the Second World War by a wandering barrage balloon that broke free from its moorings in the gasworks yard.

ALL THAT REMAINS of this part of the old town are the terraced houses to the left of these two photographs. Much of the land that was taken up by the church, school and gasworks is today occupied by chemical giants Rohm & Haas, who have manufactured in Jarrow since the 1960s (then under the name of Charles Lennig & Co.) and manufactured Oroglass (a type of Perspex) during the 1970s. The remainder of the land has been landscaped after the completion of the second road tunnel and the recently refurbished pedestrian tunnel is easily accessible from this point. This Tyne crossing opened in 1951 and has served two communities on both sides of the river for the past sixty years. In excess of 20,000 pedestrians and cyclists used the tunnel daily, via escalators, in the 1950s and '60s when industry flourished on both sides of the Tyne. The ferry service that operated from Jarrow to Howdon within the same complex was discontinued in 1967 after the completion of the road tunnel.

ST BEDE'S CHURCH

THE OLDER PHOTOGRAPH of St Bede's church dates from 1900, and was taken from the foot of Albert Road where it meets St John's Terrace. The railings to the left of the picture surrounded the Wesleyan church of St John, built in 1870. St Bede's was erected nine years earlier, in 1861, to cater for the needs of the growing Roman Catholic community, courtesy of Father Edmund Kelly who inaugurated the parish.

THE BUILDING TO the right of the church in the older of these two images was the Chapel Road School, which was added to the church in 1868. This was the first Roman Catholic school solely for girls, as the church believed these girls would provide a pool of pupil teachers to meet the future needs of the town's Roman Catholic population. This was due to an influx of Irish immigrant workers who were attracted to the town and what it had to offer. The more recent view of the church remains almost identical to its counterpart with the exception of the adjoining school building which was demolished during the 1970s in favour of a more modern building in Staple Road. This in turn was demolished in 2006. The children are now taught in St Bede's Primary School in Harold Street. This part of Albert Road no longer exists, as can be seen in the modern image.

STANLEY STREET

WAR DAMAGE CAUSED many unwelcome alterations to parts of Jarrow. Dunn Street School, pictured below in 1955, suffered serious damage and was all but flattened in an air attack during the Second World War. Local residents rallied unsuccessfully in an attempt to save the school, but their pleas were to fall upon deaf ears and the school was deemed dangerous and beyond repair. It was subsequently demolished with the exception of one prefabricated building. The authorities – right from day one in 1870, after the introduction of the Elementary Education Act – were committed

to providing a good education for the children of Jarrow. The country's first board school opened in Jarrow in 1872 and was governed by the Hedworth, Monkton and Jarrow school board, who installed certificated teacher John Witter as headmaster. Today the scene has changed considerably: the old prefab was demolished during the 1960s and replaced with a more modern establishment.

BUILT IN THE 1960s, this more modern establishment, erected close to the original, retained the name of Dunn Street Primary School. On 25 January 2003, a malicious arson attack severely damaged the building, rendering it unsafe. This senseless act of vandalism meant that the authorities were forced to make alternative arrangements for the continuation of the children's education in various schools within the town centre. The majority of the building was beyond repair, resulting in partial demolition. The school was rebuilt at considerable expense, and today the children are taught in bright and airy classrooms.

CENTRAL JARROW, LOOKING SOUTH

THE JARROW SKYLINE has changed considerably over the years and it is only when we see it from an elevated position and viewpoint that this becomes evident. The accompanying photographs – so very different, yet still similar – were taken forty years apart, just after the opening of the Tyne Tunnel in 1967 and again in 2008 at the beginning of the construction of the sister tunnel.

Everything in the foreground of the 1967 image has been demolished, with the exception of the building in the centre. This former residence and business premises was built in 1912 by Henry Abel, a pork butcher of German origin. The houses in the front foreground and to the right are the Festival Flats referred to earlier, and were demolished in 1982. The flat-roofed building to the left was that of Lewis Botto turf accountants who had many outlets in various parts of the town.

THE BIG OLD house now partially obscured by the trees in the centre of the more modern image changed ownership during the 1970s and became a Chinese takeaway. Today it serves the community as a fish and chip shop. The photographs were taken from the roof of Monastery Court, one of Jarrow's three tower blocks of flats dating from the mid 1960s, and show the tunnel entrance quite clearly in the centre of both images, and the A19 trunk road winding its way south in the distance.

HIBERNIAN ROAD

TOWARDS THE END of the Second World War most towns and cities in the country were recovering from the effects, and attempting to get back on their feet. Jarrow was no exception. Perhaps it took a bit longer for Jarrow, as it had not quite recovered from the misery of the 1930s Depression or from the terrible stigma of the Jarrow Crusade. Rationing had been in place throughout the war years and was now coming to an end in 1954, the same year as this quaint little photograph of Hibernian Road was taken. Comestibles were beginning to reappear on shelves once again, along with a plentiful supply of everyday requisites. John McLean was a second-hand furniture dealer with a showroom in Market Square and his delivery van appears in the older of these two images. The tiny cramped terraced cottages were demolished soon after the photograph was taken.

THERE WERE MANY shops in Jarrow dealing in second-time-around goods during the lean years. John McLean relocated to the former Burton Tailoring building in Ormonde Street, where the firm traded until the 1970s, this time vending new furniture and carpets as the town and its people became more affluent. The days of second-hand shops were numbered. Today we see a revival of shops selling used clothing etc., only this time these outlets are known as charity shops.

71

ALBERT ROAD

THE PRESENCE OF the telegraph poles in this image of Albert Road from 1900 signifies a degree of wealth in this part of town, as very few residents had a telephone at their disposal. It wasn't until the late 1950s and early 1960s that these luxuries became affordable and eventually a necessity. This was made possible after the introduction of the GPO telephone exchange situated in St John's Terrace. Another suggestion that this was an affluent area is the presence of well-dressed children posing for the camera to the left of the photograph. Conclusive evidence that this smart railed-off Victorian Terrace of houses was occupied by professional people is revealed within the pages of Ward's Directory of the period.

ALTHOUGH THE RAILINGS
have long since disappeared, the
houses remain exactly as they did
more than 100 years ago. Today
the old-fashioned telegraph poles
have also disappeared, and have
been replaced with satellites,
fibre-optic cables and all
manner of modern technology
by companies specialising in
telecommunications.

WEST PARK

JARROW IN THE nineteenth century was fortunate enough to have wealthy business people who took the welfare of the town and its people to their hearts. Charles Palmer in particular was benevolent to the town in many ways and another, William Richardson, was instrumental in the formation of an organised education system. Although Cuthbert Ellison is more attributed to Hebburn than Jarrow, he also owned a considerable amount of land in the town. Another of these unsung heroes of the era has to be Walter Charles James. Among the many

generous gifts he bestowed upon the town was the Ellison School and playing fields we know today as the West Park. His first association with Jarrow was after his marriage to Sarah Caroline, daughter of Cuthbert Ellison, when he inherited the enviable title of Lord Northbourne. The well-appointed drinking fountain at the park's entrance in this photograph from around 1900 was a gift to the town courtesy of baker and confectioner Thomas Sheldon. As with most of the parkland in Jarrow, West Park was used extensively during the summer months. Among its recreation facilities was a beautifully ornate Victorian bandstand, tennis courts, paddling pool and meticulously manicured bowling greens.

GREEN BOWLING HAS always been a popular pastime since the park opened in 1876 and since 1894 it has played host to many local and national bowling competitions. The paddling pool and tennis courts have long since gone, but the main body of the council-run park is very well cared for with acres of green belt and beautiful floral displays in spring and summer.

JARROW CRUSADE

AFTER THE CLOSURE of Palmer's in 1934, Jarrow was a troubled town. Eighty per cent of the town's male working population was out of work with the figure expected to rise, and rise it did, peaking at 88 per cent in 1935. The morale of the town was at an all time low, with little or no prospects. The sudden closure of Palmer's robbed the town of its lifeblood and independence. The popular MP for Jarrow at the time was Ellen Wilkinson, who recognised the seriousness of the situation and endeavoured to resolve the matter. Her first task was to address the massive unemployment problem and in 1936, with the backing of the council, set about organising the Jarrow Crusade. Two hundred of the town's fittest men were chosen to walk to London in a desperate bid for work, and to lobby Parliament. The march to the capital was all in vain as the men returned home dejected and disillusioned at the government's abrupt refusal of help. The turning point for Jarrow came after the Second World War. The inauguration of the Bede Industrial Estate in 1948

attracted many companies who recognised a ready-made workforce and were prepared to employ it in manufacturing their wares. The people of Jarrow looked forward to prosperity and a brighter future. The pedestrian tunnel opened in 1951, which brought with it better prospects of work on both sides of the river.

JARROW TODAY IS a bright, modern, go-ahead town, resurrected from the dark days of a dismal past. It is now time for the people to walk in the sunshine and not under the canopy of the Depression of the 1930s. These photographs show the Jarrow Crusade departing the town in 1936 on their epic journey to the capital, and the modern-day bronze sculpture 'Spirit of Jarrow' by Graham Ibbeson, commemorating this milestone in the town's colourful past.

NORTH STREET

BRANCHES OF THE country's four major banks of the era were in Ellison Street. Martin's Bank was amalgamated into the Barclays Group, and close by is NatWest. The Trustee Savings Bank vacated

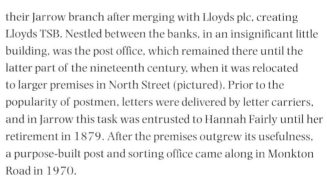

their Jarrow branch after merging with Lloyds plc, creating Lloyds TSB. Nestled between the banks, in an insignificant little building, was the post office, which remained there until the latter part of the nineteenth century, when it was relocated to larger premises in North Street (pictured). Prior to the popularity of postmen, letters were delivered by letter carriers, and in Jarrow this task was entrusted to Hannah Fairly until her retirement in 1879. After the premises outgrew its usefulness, a purpose-built post and sorting office came along in Monkton Road in 1970.

TODAY, THE SORTING office remains, but the counter service was relocated to within the Presto supermarket during the 1980s; it is currently situated in Grange Road. Up until 1960 Jarrow and Hebburn Co-operative Society were prevalent in this busy street. The white building closest to the camera was a department store, while the next building supported individual units on the ground floor. The first floor of the building, the 'store hall' as it was affectionately known, was used as a dance venue and a place for children's parties. The whole area was cleared over the forthcoming years, and became this swanky new housing estate.

GRANGE ROAD

AS RECOLLECTIONS OF the hardship of the war years faded into the history books, some of our towns fared better than others as they were released from the scourge of food rationing. For Jarrow, it was around 1954 when the light appeared at the end of what seemed to be a very dark and never-ending tunnel. It is only in modern times that the majority of the perishable goods we purchase are wrapped in clear film, or vacuum packed in difficult-to-open plastic bubbles. This is a far cry from the way it was presented in the good old days, when butter was patted for you as you required it, and sugar was weighed and served in blue bags. A small proportion of grocers in town

were part of multiple organisations, similar to Hanlon's and Lipton's, but there were plenty of opportunities for the independent grocer, thirty-nine of them in fact, who earned a good living vending fresh produce here up until the late 1950s. Amos Hinton, one of the country's leading grocers, traded in Western Road in one of its ninety-two countrywide branches. Gallon's, Hadrian and Duncan's were alternate suppliers of comestibles in both pre- and post-war years. Eventually these companies merged during the 1970s, creating Allied Foods Ltd. This charming photograph typifies a Saturday morning in busy Grange Road in 1950. Soon after the photograph was taken, everything in it was demolished as part of the council's redevelopment programme.

NOT ONLY DID the buildings disappear, but most importantly, the character of this part of town disappeared along with them, which becomes evident as we look at the modern-day equivalent above.

THE ROYAL OAK

IN 1801, APPROXIMATELY the same time as Simon Temple was preparing to surface the first coal from the infamous Alfred Pit, Jarrow's population numbered a mere 1,600. Ten years on, it

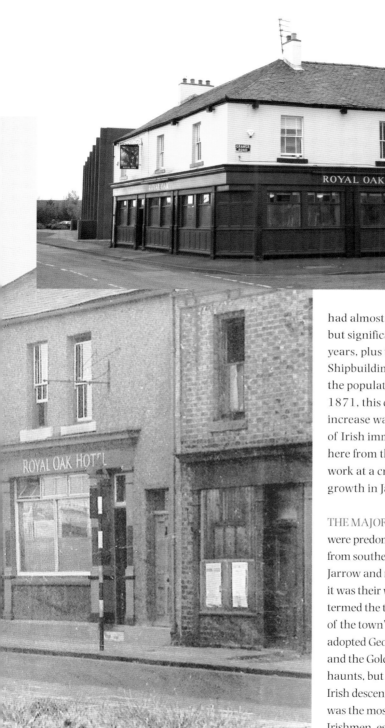

had almost doubled to 3,140. A steady but significant rise in the subsequent years, plus the advent of the Palmer Shipbuilding Empire in 1851, swelled the population to almost 25,000. By 1871, this continual yet sustained increase was partially due to an influx of Irish immigrant workers who came here from the Emerald Isle seeking work at a crucial time of industrial growth in Jarrow.

THE MAJORITY OF these immigrants were predominantly Roman Catholics from southern Ireland, who settled in Jarrow and made it their home, and it was their welcome presence which termed the town 'Little Ireland'. Several of the town's hostelries welcomed the adopted Geordies. The Crown & Anchor and the Golden Lion were popular haunts, but Kitty Monroe, a publican of Irish descent who owned the Royal Oak was the most popular landlady with the Irishmen, especially on St Patrick's Day.

PALMER STREET

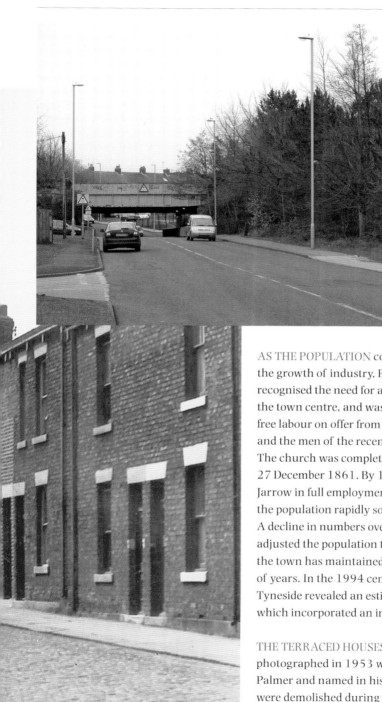

AS THE POPULATION continued to rise alongside the growth of industry, Father Edmund Kelly recognised the need for a Roman Catholic church in the town centre, and was to take advantage of the free labour on offer from the newly arrived Irishmen and the men of the recently formed parish of St Bede. The church was completed and officially opened on 27 December 1861. By 1891, with the people of Jarrow in full employment in all manner of industry, the population rapidly soared to an amazing 52,000. A decline in numbers over the subsequent years adjusted the population to around 30,000, a figure the town has maintained for a considerable number of years. In the 1994 census the Borough of South Tyneside revealed an estimated figure of 156,700, which incorporated an input of 27,000 from Jarrow.

THE TERRACED HOUSES of Palmer Street as photographed in 1953 were constructed by Charles Palmer and named in his honour in 1875. They were demolished during the eventful 1950s, and the land lay derelict for many years until the popularity of industrial parks during the 1970s. The land is now occupied by factories.

CHAPEL ROAD

IN THE 1950S, television in Jarrow was still quite rare, and was certainly a luxury affordable to few privileged families. At this time the majority of homes were illuminated by gas and it wasn't until later in the decade that houses were converted to electricity or were being constructed with it installed. The introduction of electricity opened up new horizons, as refrigerators and a wide assortment of modern-day appliances appeared for domestic use. From as early as 1900 some of our streets had been illuminated by electricity, but this was limited to the main thoroughfares of the town, and gas remained the principal source of illumination. When the older of these two images was taken in 1954, Chapel Road was the shortest and most direct link between Monkton Road and Ellison Street, and was quite a heavily populated area.

NOWADAYS IT IS unrecognisable, as everything has been demolished with the exception of the Crown & Anchor public house, which has served ale since Victorian times. Chapel Road today is nothing more than an access road for the shopping centre and parking facilities.

LONGMORE MEMORIAL FOUNTAIN

GREEN BELT AREAS solely for the purpose of recreation were created just out of town at Primrose. The Temperance Ground became known as Springwell Park, where rose beds and sunken Italian gardens flourished and were a feature of what were formerly cornfields. The Longmore drinking fountain (pictured) was relocated here from the town centre in 1921.

Erected in Ellison Street in 1891, the fountain was paid for by public subscription and dedicated to the memory of Joseph Longmore, who passed away in 1890 aged forty-nine. Longmore was a founder member of the Venerable Bede Lodge for the sons of Temperance; he was also president of the Band of Hope. The Temperance Ground upon which it was situated was thought to be appropriate, and stood as a tribute befitting a man so heavily involved within the Temperance movement. These grounds were purchased by the council from the widow of paper mill owner and Quaker, William Henry Richardson of Monkton Lodge after his death in 1923, and were swiftly converted into the park.

AS THE YEARS passed, the rose beds and sunken gardens that it once boasted suffered through acts of vandalism and were eventually disbanded along with the tennis courts. Richardson's former home, Monkton Lodge, survives and serves the community as the Branches nursing home in Springwell Road. The park remains today, sheltered with avenues of well-established trees.

JARROW PAPER MILL

WHILE THERE IS evidence of coal mining in Jarrow from as early as 1618, coal surfacing didn't get under way commercially until shipyard owner Simon Temple began extracting from the Alfred Pit in 1803. Due to the lack of health and safety regulations, tragedy was never far away from the troubled mine. Many lives were lost as a result of working very long hours at the coal face in a combustible environment. Another volatile industry in Jarrow which was susceptible to outbursts of fire was the paper manufacturing at the mills in Springwell. From its inauguration in 1841 to its

demise in 1928, no fewer than twenty-seven major fires were recorded and attended by firemen from Monkton, Gateshead and Jarrow. Vast quantities of esparto grass, necessary in this type of paper making, were stored in outbuildings separated from the main body of the mill, and were vulnerable to combustion. The mill lay derelict for five years until the newly formed Jarrow Instruction Centre (JIC) utilised the buildings from 1935 to teach new skills to the recently unemployed men of the town after the unexpected collapse of Palmer's works. The centre was disbanded at the outbreak of the Second World War, and the decaying mill was abandoned yet again.

DURING THE 1960s, these buildings were used for furniture storage, and later by Kenton Utilities. Eventually the site was cleared and the land reclaimed for use as a private housing estate. These images show the remnants of the former mill, and the detatched residences of Mill Dene View that replaced it.

MONASTERY RUINS

IT WAS THE Anglo Saxons who reoccupied a first century Roman fort on the site of Jarrow in the fifth century, when there had been many derivations of the name which was recorded around AD 750 as 'Gyruum' and 'Gyrwy', meaning 'marsh dwellers' from the Anglo Saxon word 'gyr' which translates to 'mud' or 'marsh'. Other spellings were also discovered, such as 'Jaruum' in 1158 and 'Jarwe' in 1228. Notice how similar these words are to what the Jarovians refer to the town as today: 'Jarra'. The monastery of St Paul was one half of a twin foundation (the other was St Peter's at Wearmouth). Bede was installed with the 600 brothers

at the Jarrow monastery at the age of twelve, and remained there until his death from asthma aged sixty-two on 26 May AD 735. When the monastery was founded in AD 685, it was reputed to be the only centre of learning north of Rome – effectively the first university in England – and attracted scholars from Europe and beyond. The Viking raids on the two monasteries at Wearmouth and Jarrow inflicted serious damage; the damage to Jarrow was so severe that it had to be abandoned and it lay desolate for 150 years. In AD 1075, Aldwine, Ealfwin and Kinfrid were sent by Walcher, bishop of Durham to restore the monastery but were unsuccessful.

AS THE CENTURIES passed, further attempts were made to repair the crumbling cloisters, which by this time had suffered irreparable damage. The Roman and Saxon remains have lain undisturbed for many centuries.

CLAYTON STREET

ANOTHER EXAMPLE OF Charles Mark
Palmer's generosity was the construction
of a hospital in Clayton Street within
the town centre. The Palmer Memorial
Hospital was erected in 1870 in memory
of his first wife, Jane. It was originally
designed for the welfare of his workforce,
who subscribed to its upkeep at the rate
of 2d per week per person. While the
workforce and officialdom agreed to the
2d levy, it was thought by some to be
excessive. Nevertheless the charge was
implemented on the realisation that health
issues in such a volatile industry were
of paramount importance, and the fact
that lives could be endangered if medical
help had to be sought further afield. After
the closure of Palmer's yard in 1934,
the Board of Health presided over the
day-to-day running of the hospital until
1947 and the introduction of the National

Health Service. Eventually the ailing building became too costly to maintain, and as a consequence was demolished in the late 1970s in favour of a modern establishment, which was built on the site of the original in the 1980s, bearing the Palmer name, as the Palmer Community Hospital.

THE ORIGINAL BUILDING displayed a magnificent stained-glass window at its entrance, which was preserved, and is displayed once again within the confines of the new building. These two contrasting images show part of the original hospital directly behind the Palmer statue to the left of the 1910 photograph, and the hospital as it is today.

Other titles published by The History Press

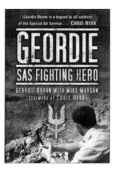

Geordie: SAS Fighting Hero
GEORDIE DORAN WITH MIKE MORGAN, FOREWORD BY CHRIS RYAN

Geordie Doran ranks as one of the most remarkable fighting soldiers of the twentieth century. Growing up in Jarrow during the Depression years of the 1930s, Geordie signed up as a private soldier in 1946 and embarked on a career spanning 40 years. He saw active service in Germany, Cyprus, the Korean War and Suez; he became an expert in jungle warfare in Malaya and in Borneo, as well as on key special operations in the deserts of Oman and Yemen, and Colonel Gaddafi's Libya.

978 0 7524 6053 6

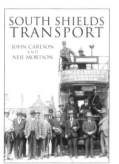

South Shields Transport
JOHN CARLSON AND NEIL MORTSON

Roughly moving around the town along the old 'figure of eight' electric tram route that opened in 1906, this book rediscovers the lost world of the horse-drawn and electric trams through to trolleybuses and motorbuses operated by South Shields Corporation Transport. The Corporation boasted that there was no part of the town that was more than a quarter of an hour's walk away from this route.

978 0 7524 4222 8

Ghostly Tyne & Wear
ROB KIRKUP

From reports of haunted castles, pubs, theatres and shopping arcades, to heart-stopping accounts of apparitions, poltergeists and related supernatural phenomena, this book investigates thirty of the most haunted locations in Tyne & Wear today. Illustrated with over sixty photographs, together with location and access details for each location, this book is sure to appeal all those interested in finding out more about the area's haunted heritage.

978 0 7509 5109 8

The Great Siege of Newcastle, 1644
ROSIE SERDIVILLE AND JOHN SADLER

In the autumn of 1644 was fought one of the most sustained and desperate sieges of the First Civil War, when Scottish Covenanter forces under the Earl of Leven finally stormed Newcastle-upon-Tyne, the King's greatest bastion in the north-east and the key to his power there. The book tells the story of the people who fought there, what motivated them and who led them there. It is also an account of what happened on the day, a minute-by-minute chronicle of Newcastle's bloodiest battle.

978 0 7524 5989 9

Visit our website and discover thousands of other History Press books.

www.thehistorypress.co.uk